Leaving Nothing Behind

Martin Willitts Jr.

Fernwood
PRESS

Leaving Nothing Behind

©2023 by Martin Willitts Jr.

Fernwood Press
Newberg, Oregon
www.fernwoodpress.com

Printed in the United States of America

Page design: Mareesa Fawver Moss
Cover art: Minerva Miller

ISBN 978-1-59498-110-4

Dedicated to my wife, Linda Griggs

Contents

Introduction

"Every time I plant the perennials ..." writes the speaker of these poems, "I'm leaving a part of me immortal" (This Is Why I Plant Perennials). In this book of soil and seasons, Martin Willitts has painted that inconceivable place where the temporal and eternal meet, where time is suspended and the natural order surrenders itself—for a moment—to faith in the unknowable. Here, the air is weeping, water dreams, leaves breathe, ash laments, and light embodies a variety of movements and reflections concerning how the speaker interacts with subtle changes in his environment.

Poetry, for some, is a literature of solace and hope. We lean into its lyrical language to feel our inner longings for connection and insight. Willitts offers this in these poems as his speaker searches his surroundings for signs of renewal and comfort; as he bends over the flowers in his garden to discover their openness seeking "an access where the heart escapes" (Healing in the Field); as he sketches "the memory of love" revealed in "turquois wildflowers" (Field Study); as he experiences a sense of belonging in the forest imbued with the "Presence" of a higher power (The Calling); as he learns to be quiet, lowering his heart "like a stone

/ in molasses filling the emptiness" (Sitting Still to Hear Quiet).

These picturesque moments lend themselves to larger themes of aging and coming to terms with loss. According to the speaker of these poems, our lives are earthly and connected to natural elements, but they are also part of a parallel spiritual universe. If the speaker is still enough, the poems suggest, he can discover impressions of the spiritual in this temporal world. He can connect with God, defined as *infinite love* and *silence*, and wonder at the way the world bears witness to something beyond. In these poems, nothing is ever really lost.

But these poems do not romanticize reality; rather, they take note of pain and suffering while setting these realities within a universal program of hope. In other words, the speaker feels deep concern for a neighbor who "has first stage melanoma" while he is simultaneously comforted by the sight of geese who fly off "into *forever*" in the same way he believes the spirit of a man or woman will eventually lift into eternity—a place of constant comfort.

And some of the most beautiful poems in this collection address simple human interactions between the speaker and those he loves who have already suffered their own losses. For instance, in "The Day is Speechlessly Broken," he uses his hands to create a silent language for his deaf father, signing "*songbirds*" as they walk outside. And, in "Amazing Grace," he reminisces about how his Amish grandmother, who denounced singing, was caught singing the old hymn because she, like all of us, harbored a "hidden voice" needing to be released as though "her life depended upon it / as if everyone needed grace." These are poignant, human moments—moments that reveal how much we need one another as well as our cravings for a sound, a sign, a companion to lift our spirits season by season.

Willitts applies brush stroke after brush stroke with each poem, referring to impressionist paintings and scientific names of birds and flora throughout to usher his reader into a garden filled with the wild and domestic, where time is suspended and we can experience layers of life—temporal and eternal, earthly and spiritual, the possible and the impossible—unveiling before us. We can see where these worlds kiss and play like "light forever chasing light" (Leaving Nothing Behind). We can even enter into the "end of life / fearless / unburdened" knowing that even in death we will continue to share a "unique music" as we "let go" and become a sustaining part of the ever-evolving universe (Music). We become part of the whole symphony and canvas. Nothing is truly left behind.

Kimberly Ann Priest
author of *Slaughter the One Bird*

I. This Is How Light Works

"I would like to paint the way a bird sings."
Claude Monet

Leaving Nothing Behind

Waterlilies (*Nymphaeaceae*)

The lily appreciates the passage of time.
It rises from below water to surface at first light,
turning to face light, rotating to search
through leaf cover and cloud blockage,
descending back into water at night
like a watchman finishing his shift, punching out.

On the watercolor pond, the lilies are scrolls
opening to record daily moments;
nothing gets by them unnoticed. At the end of day,
they crumple like tissue paper, their messages
still orbiting inside.

A maple leaf journeys down
as a distant afterthought,
deciding to stay and comment, settling
within the arc of twilight.

Thousands of words,
like metallic-blue dragonflies,
have passed along the edge
of this pond, skimming effortlessly on the thin skin,
then settling into a splash,
as the pond takes everything inside itself.

Two late raindrops land on the surface, enter
a circle,
and merge.

Light is forever chasing light.

I stand out as the only one out of place—
I am not a pine needle, nor locust throb, or raspberry,
nor heron taking off with disturbed restlessness.

Light

Light burrows out of darkness.
Our skin is covered with silvery sheen
like cherries polished by spring rain.
The terribly hard days flood by—
gone to where they are not needed anymore.

Light finds us through layers of clothes,
woolen blankets, cool sheets
smelling of orange-sunshine. Light
always finds the hidden and exposes it.

Our hair reminds light of damp earth
when buds first break free
in rapture—they cannot wait
or cannot get enough of it.

God is no longer untouchable.
We are cleansed. Our bones
are transitory voices, flocking geese
practicing for that long journey
to an end they cannot imagine—
but there it is, the end in sight,
calling from the distance,
Come here, come here,
I am waiting for you.

We reach what we have been reaching for,
and it is more than we expected it to be.

Transformation

Light changes slowly with subtle words
such as *cautious* and *determined*,
marking a demarcation line across the horizon,
delineating between day and night
taking over the sky. Drakes in the wetlands
are excited by the transformation.

In daylight, the moon is a white wafer.
Perception only amazes
the participant who never notices
the daily occurrences with minor variations.

What difference are the blending shades,
clouds wheeling like hawks, the way light
haunches on the edge while day begins or ends.
There is always this anticipation of the differences,
and the end results are that our expectations are met—

not in color or uncertain times for the transfers
but in the way no two days begin or end the same.
For thousands of years, the universe has palpitated,
expanded, and contracted like a heart
with such restlessness we barely notice
what is plain to the eye: the universe is constant
and changeable. We barely break the surface
of observation, and when we do, we take for granted
the drakes will migrate when marshes are ice-tinged,
and the drakes will return when spring returns,
never considering it might be otherwise.

Daffodils in Light

(Narcissus poeticus)

I planted the daffodils in early fall,
never thinking much about it.
Having planted so many fall seasons,
one year fell away from another.

During the year, you died.
I thought too much of it—
all we never did together;
it was too late to get more days back.

Sooner or later, grief buried itself deeper
and deeper. My heart needed rest.
There is a love that tears us to pieces
like yellow petals of grief.

And then one day, minding my business,
I pass by where the daffodils were.
I remembered that you had loved them,
and you came back to me.

Do not say second chances are not possible;
surely as one daffodil is different than another,
each launching silent boats of forgiveness,
anything is possible.

Reflected Shade and Hint of Light

Based on Monet's numerous paintings of *Water Lilies*

we need to work quickly
before light changes

it is fickle
dashing about
nakedly
in a drifting manner

nothing is this frantic

not the previous loss of hair
or woodpecker rattling an elm

drifting light must be seized
or it is lost
it will never be the same

gold and purple
dimness
or luminescence
of faint flowers
teasing paint

I identify with this

the water lilies tell me
paint fast
their pistils licking the edged darkness

my hands become light
glowing lush as greening pools

as eyelashes flinch
and ripple

Burning

Violets (*Viola sororia*)

A wave of violets near me
are tiny as raindrops.
There seems to be light all around them.

There is a night-forest of fireflies,
incandescent lights, shaking and fluctuating,
trying to attract a mate, showing the way to love—

burning like violet suns dying into exhaustion
because of their short available time
before vanishing.

We have only so long to make a permanent statement.
Are we doing all we can
with the little time we have?

Within Reach of Purpose

"...wild is anything / beyond the reach of purpose not its own."
Wendell Berry

I actively search for wilderness
like a musician studies a score
to know tempo and rest spots.

I could study the wild for hours
with cameras or microscopes or telescopes
or notebooks or using empirical studies
with four-square analysis like a researcher,
never seeing the same experience twice,

trying to understand love
or death or how two similar seeds
grow two different flowers.

Healing in the Field

Here, light opens the only gate
to a field of clear vision
among the dissonant whir
of katydids. The body of Silence is moving.

What seemed out of reach
was not dulled senses
nor tarnished light
nor tongues of marigolds
but enforced *openness*—an access
where the heart escapes, where
rightness of the experience assembles
into recognition,
exhausted at Silence's feet.

Our arms are heavy-tired
from lifting so much light
into our hearts of loss.

The Sky Is Wide and Needs Filling

Skylark (*Alauda arvensis*) and trillium
or wake robin (*Trillium grandiflorum*)

A skylark by the trillium
takes off after feeling noticed.

Its wings are soft thunder
never reaching full distance.

The world is startling and indifferent,
raining green into cracked red clay.

A trillium is fighting to avoid
its last days that are yawning before it.

Loose dirt blows in tiny dust devils,
but the trillium does not cringe.

The skylark cannot be seen,
so it is easily forgotten.

The skylark vanishes into the *impossible*.
The trillium is receiving necessary rain.

The storm creaks toward its last breath.
A few downed trees are split uncomfortably.

I could look out thousands of windows
and never see this intersection of time.

A part of me is in the far-off where skylarks go.
I only wish I could be there, too.

Messages

The last line of geese has drumming wings
across a wintery sky.
Clouds begin parting
like alchemy.

I get to witness this each year,
knowing they will return
like cherry blossoms or laughter or
the magic of a found raven feather.

These last greening days
do not need to be explained.

Crossing Over

Trees grow straight on slopes,
finding light. Light arrives later
for the ones below:
white birch with its buckling bark,
hollowed-out silver maple,
and the firs that never find their way
and cannot muscle toward the light.

These dull leaves on the ground
seem never composed into a leaving.

This slope comes to a stream,
more of an afterthought
than anything a beaver could use.

If you follow a stream, sooner or later
you get somewhere. But for now,
we cross to the other side,
barely getting our shoes wet.

You cannot hear water this shallow.
It does not seem right.

The lack of sound is not normal.
The forest is holding its breath
like a person in deep meditation.

The land flattens into another silence,
its chest barely moving. Here,
trees darken as black walnut.
The little bank is mostly small rocks.
Not one bird is anywhere.
It does not seem right to be so quiet.

Crossing from one side
to another is like moving between
two unalike worlds, crossing
a clear division from life to death.

Nature does not consider what is right;
it only does what it needs to do.

Field Study

In the threshold of a field,
wading birds find water,
unwavering.

I bring a sketch pad and pencil
to study the memory of love,
the skin of leaves,
turquoise wildflowers,
birds breaking into shadows.

Water is dreaming,
wavering tree reflections,
where truth is distorted
as memory,
sprout heron wings.

A frog extends its legs, pushing water
like a woman emptying bird songs.

Dipping My Hand into a Cold Lake

I touch the lake, and it flinches—
discord music
like a colliding rock slide.

Elsewhere, ripples cause
the sun to explode,
and we wouldn't be alive to see it
missing eons from now.

My reflection wrinkles
into a choreograph
as time shimmers
the Aurora Borealis.

When I touch my finger to the water,
I never expect the startling.

At night, my dreams are all watery,
translucent as piano chords,
and I am one of those notes.

Seeking the Invisible

The disquieting before a storm
suspends between canopies.
Darkening leaves
the swirled land.

Little in this world is absolute.

Rain topples
on the contour of earth,
easing the stultifying heat.

We knew it was coming
by the surge.

It will pass,
memory or errant words,
leaving behind some chaos.

The earth wants what it wants.

It wants what we cannot see.

On This Summer Day

Morning is ponderous
as cows in interceding rain.

In this light,
words of encouragement are hard to find.

Waterlilies wait to rise from below the surface,
telling us it will be alright: this, too, will pass.

Extreme light unfolds
its white petals toward more light,

storing it for later, shushes of calm,
breath assembling what we will need:

so much penetrating light—
numbing us into meditative silence—

I am frightened by the possibility
I will never see you again.

I cannot write what I cannot say.
It is quiet when you're not here

or anywhere.
Rain is writing this down.

The weight of this morning is heavy,
when, in a blink, you go away.

Making

Now is the time of quiet interlude
where small branches bud and break.
I try willing them into Being now.

When they do,
they take their own sweet time,
music building into a crescendo.

Even in emptiness, small buds
are determined to make leaves.
All of this cannot be seen.

When you finally notice it,
you do not know what to say.
It is already said in the making.

This Is How Light Works Where It Is Darkest

Based on the painting, *Waterlilies, Green Reflection, Left Part,*
by Claude Monet, 1916

This is how light works:

it is a woman holding her head
upon the surface tension of a pond
as it supports her weight on its fleshy skin.
She is as weightless as lilies,
her face rippling concentric circles of color.

This is how light moves:

it affects the sounds of color—
a newborn,
its heartbeat floats, a trail of dark into light.
When I lift green from the lily pad into my hands,
it is your whisper.

Light drifts from my heart.
It is all I could do not to float away on that water.

That first birth of light and that last futile light
matter most.
Everything else is clouds reflected on green waters
mirrored in the clouds,
changing when light changes.
Lilies hear this change.

In between is the throb of fireflies.

This is when light becomes a fugue of silence,
cutting the embryo cord,
unmooring lily pads.

This is how light works:

we are interconnected with everything in the universe—
each dark fragment, each strand of love—
so when we swim toward death,
we are never alone.

When someone holds our memory,
we are never gone.
We are a part of the whole.
We are a part of the clouds, the cricket's music,
the white light from the lily, the green
births, the halting heartbeats—
so that where it is darkest,
it is always light.

When I hold you
like it might be the last time I hold you,
we are light.

Molecules

Light is not lush nor mute
nor even a combination of ghosts
rising from a carpet
as a funnel of dust motes,
visible, exposed.
They have always been there;
we're just finally noticing them.

This world consists of molecules,
even the light, dust, and ink on this paper.

II. Change Is About to Break

"The best way to know God is to love many things."
Vincent van Gogh

Change Is About to Break

The sky is diaphanous. Someone points out the obvious—
what little we have is permanent. It is never enough.
Unresolved parts from the past extend to the future,
sometimes summoning the worst in us,
turning anger into a blunt instrument.

We hold the emptiness of unfulfilled promises,
unable to move ahead. We question
without receiving answers. Light barely emerges
over the horizon, fleetingly, almost refusing to appear.
We ache for that warmth. It has been a long winter,
and only desire remains, ebbing. Sensing a break,
hidden birds are chittering excitedly.

That one sprung-free moment whispers
to ignore those distractions heading our way.
Memory will fiddle around, transcribing and editing,
from second to second, until completely re-arranged.

Revelation

It begins with some simple light
reflecting off an unglazed red clay pot.
There is some strangeness about that light
or the utter basic nature of the pot
or earthen source of the clay
or the forming of intense heat in the kiln
or faltering coals expended into ash
that made this revelation
possible and necessary, opened
the invisible gateway to the Creator,
whose name changes from religion to religion
like a chameleon, while the Creator
remains both the same and flexible.

I had not noticed—but now, my eyes blend
dirt spun into a clay pot, light
coming great distances to glance off that pot
as simple and basic as air in the swirl of dust.

But it is not just one revelation; it is many—
the prism of light, the earth we take for granted,
the purpose of fire to create, the voiceless God,
the white baby breath flowers lasting two months:
all things possible and impossible.

The Distant Calling

Days come faster, sooner,
a river of geese over a lake,
one reflecting the other, one leaving
while the other cannot travel any further.

I cannot grasp the days.
When I do, they flap crazily,
birds shedding white greasy feathers,
trying to escape.

There is something about leaving
this world behind and something
about staying—
both are necessary.

I feel I'm about to lose it all—

this world, this imperfect me,
this urge to depart, and this call to stay,
this river of silence moving more quickly.

I hear the distant calling.

I am holding back.
My pulse quickens.

Are the geese returning or leaving
or circling
or waiting for me to join?

Counting the Days

The burdened trees at the beginning of day
bent more, bent
lower, like a person tired after a hard day,
striving for an impossible goal,
knowing the search must carry on
to another day.

Small moments gather, tiny details—
like the randomness of common grackles
composing on the ground,
pricking their tails in the headwinds.

Not even snow flurries
unbundling out of nowhere
deterred those birds
from rushing headlong
into the empty tree branches,
bending light.

That noise,
then silence—
both were quick notations.

Held in the Light

Because there is a difference between sunlight
and God's healing Light, this poem is for those
needing wellness.

Because we should be listening,
we might be healed from the hidden voice
holding us within the Light.

These are promises meant to be kept.

Because we are complicit in our own joy
or misery, this poem is intended to extend love—
even if no one wants it. The Light does not
hang back from finding you,
your hidden desire to be seen.

Light is unrelenting.
We need to walk within such blessings.

Notice:
light is pouring out of our bodies.
It is delicious and delirious in its intensity.

Notice:
we are pulsing with light, and the best part is
we don't have to think about it.

Light arrives, inhabiting us;
whatever we touch
will never be the same,
and neither will we.

We are held in arms of light.

Every Birdsong

Every time a bird tries a new song,
if it fails, it tries again.
It cannot stand silence
and wants to paint the skies with music.

The bird searches, again, for some song
no one ever heard before, so rain can lift
its heavy burden.

That song must be haunting.

It must ease the most miserable hot day,
when all anyone can do it rest.

A song could doodle
long, looping calligraphy into everywhere,
indelibly and astonishingly kinetic,
opening up
every difficult place.

Every Spring

I pry wet, brown, crinkled leaves
from the downspout, a premonition of spring.
An ash's roots extend into our yard.
I section off parts of the garden
with recycled red brick. There is much to be done,
and there is no end of it. I put my foot down
on the hoe and push. I am determined
to make something of it. *This* is my demarcation line.
This is where I will grow things. The grass,
weeds, and dandelions can have the rest.
The garden hears me coming a week away.
The ground gears up for it.
I wish I could say the same for myself.
Someday, I will be too old for this. But for now,
I'm up to the task, gauging myself,
sectioning off work, so it is less work.
Getting older and gardening,
I have learned to spread myself
as if I have all the time in the world.

Where Are the Stars Tonight?

Where are the stars tonight?
I cannot find myself in the dark.
I have never felt more alone and abandoned.

It is soundless here. I cannot find anyone
in this emptiness.
I have forgotten all I knew.

The moon is blue. The second moon in a month is
a mouth swallowing the stars.
If I move, I might disappear in the dark.

The Unfinished Symphony

The story of our lives is still being revised
and sung—yours, mine, everyone's song
is deep and curious—listen!

The hummingbird cannot imagine such music
being so serious and exciting—
it must spread the news from flower to flower,
its over-joyous news spilling like pollen.
Then, a bumblebee carries that nectar
with its calming news—

taking it, dancing almost drunkenly,
spreading it like an old-fashioned town crier,
buzzing with ecstasy, far and wide.
Small stones feel so large when hearing the news
that light breaks out of them,
adding to the generous music.

O, marvelous heart; you hear it, too!
Even the motionlessness is stirred by the news!

Even the fox with its swishing tail stops trotting,
pauses with the recent, limp chicken
in its curled mouth. It remembers as a kit
frolicking in the last blossoms after a monarch,
trying to nip it. Even the fox sighs,
humming with forgotten pleasure.
Yes, even the fox heard the song being sung, too.

Yes, even the old woman, huddling in a quilt,
trying to maintain a little bit of warmth
in the dayroom light, hears this song.
Even though she is
considered too old and empty of memory—
yes, even she feels that unfinished symphony
of her life and smiles like bread rising—

for we are all born into this world.

Listening

A voice said, "Come, bring your notebook."
No one was there.

I heard, "Follow me."

I went without asking *why* or *where*.
I drove without knowing where I was headed.

"Stop here."

In the buttercup fields, silence and noise
were near the edge
of reoccurring dreams.

How do I begin to please an acknowledged master?
All I have are questions and the emptiness of my days.
Whatever I have been given came
like irregular rain falling from another world.

"What do you see?"

Glimpses of the wilderness,
sighs from the mesmerized deer, emanations
from a stream, helplessness being assisted
by compassion, a rider bringing psalms.

There was more going on in the background,
more than I could ever see if I had a thousand eyes.
Nothing that could put words to what I saw,

not with a million lifetimes and numerous tongues.
There is a narrow space between being overwhelmed
and incomplete. The willingness to try
balances them, imperfectly, but Hope keeps nudging,
an ecstatic voice suggesting, "Follow me."

How I Know Things Are Coming Back

Among the lupines and peonies in mid-May,
there are hidden promises of the forthcoming astilbe.
What is secure in this season?
Double columbines of blue geraniums,
reddish-purple, tiny-leaved clematis etoile violette,
pink anemones, large white trumpets
of fragrant cloud are soloing in the chorus.

But my garden is too small for my ambitions.
I have to work tight, constricted,
composing haiku of underlying colors.

If only I could've included butterscotch-gold scots pine—
the lending of structure and intricate details,
its vessel shapes of triangle ship masts. The canvas
of my garden is waiting for inspiration.
Pale white snow-in-summer spreads
on rock-edged raised beds, enjoying sunlight.
O what I could do with dusty-mulberry smokebush!

In those long spells of no supplemental watering,
in flashes of iridescence, in transporting odors,
in absentminded waiting for things to happen,
there is a challenge at imposing order where chaos was.

Planting began in earnest, in the most violent of snowstorms
when clouds rub their hands with precision,
as a constant reminder—nothing can be planned—
from the first garden where nothing was named
to this garden where nothing is too much, but it is.

Crickets

(Gryllus campestris)

While planting thick, miniature, devilish gardens
of leopard-spotted ferns in humbling silence, there
is an almost-sound my ears have nearly forgotten.
It is so small I almost missed its faint beginnings.
It takes a while for recognition to plant itself.
It is a secret I almost missed.

A cricket is singing thanks.

As the summer heat grew fierce as penance,
the cricket sings sharper and faster.
You could measure heat by its frantic clicking.
As everything cools, it slows its message.
Cricket songs carry dawn throughout night
as if songs of praise were never long enough.

And after all, isn't it what this is really all about?
This singing life, this tremble of heart and heat,
chants of simple pleasures. These sublime desires
hide in greenness with incredibly grateful singing.

Nature

We are immersed in nature, ceaselessly panting
with anticipation in the orchestra of wildflowers
for those things hidden under low-lying bushes
bringing forth the essence of fact—

all things encircle us, formed by light,
in the movement of air,
whether it is still or ruffled as a river,
where everything graces our wonderment,
smells buzzing, colors soaked in dew.
Transparent senses brush us,

either with winter hoarfrost
or southern heat
stretched out like a stroked cat
or flashes of sunlight
as dragonflies in the trembling forest.

If we ever live long enough, let us enjoy
these enflamed fluctuations of light
with trickles of indigo and absorbing blues.

April 1

There is a rumor that spring is here.
You could have fooled me.
We still have cupcakes of snow.

Underneath, there might be hidden promises
of snowdrops, the first sign of spring.
For now, all we have is the illusion of spring.

The chill has lasted over three months.
I lost count and threw away the calendar.
All I can do is wait in silence:

no crocus, no daffodil, no mourning doves,
no sound of spring, no digging trowel,
no turning of dirt, no peepers.

The air is so cold, I can hear it break.
It is exhausting to be this close, this far.
The joke seems to be on spring.

I rummage for the calendar to find answers.
The dates look like seed catalogs.
My winter coat agrees; it's too cold for spring.

Belonging

The smallest rock is a part of the beginning of the universe.
We, too, are pieces of every connection,
and without any section of the whole, the world is lacking.

I feel this loss when you are not here. I know it
in the crevasses of my skin,

                                        quail rushing.
Just as wind moves a branch of black leaves

on a mountain of snowcapped rocks
beyond the senselessness,

it is all part of the belonging and not belonging.

Listening into the Silence

In the quiet, morning is unburdened—
the sky a hibiscus color:
curious love.

Day begins.
Abundance cascades
crescendos of birdsong—
omens just a heartbeat away,

elegies of living
when we feel too much,
poised to learn what we need to know—

this inescapable realization
of entering into the marvelous!

Too soon, the moment is over.
Light understands
the unexpected, the lament,
the surrender, the cold, unsettling,
surprising force of wonder and loss.

I listen into the silence
for instructions, hoping
a voice will answer,
not from within
but from *otherworldliness*.

This Is Why I Plant Perennials

Every time I plant the perennials—
daffodils, tulips, tiger lilies, hollyhocks—
I'm leaving a part of me immortal:
my immeasurable desire.

I anticipate those first green shoots,
foreshadowing my promise to myself.
Planting is more than peace-filled,
silent meditation or renewal.

And when flowers die, falling to ground,
they will not represent eventual revival
or the promise of return, yet their seeds
are reminders of my pledges for more:

more voices, more colors, more for
someone to remember me. People
might continually travel by, commenting,
I saw him planting there—

flowers forever arriving on schedule:
daffodils, pink tulips, tiger lilies tasting
sunlight, fifteen-foot hollyhocks
looking over fences for me.

Borage

(*Borago officinalis*)
Also known as *Starflower*, used in medicine for gastrointestinal
problems

In this cobalt world, new and old life swarms.
Bees travel impossible distances to these
blue-gray florets; the air is dark with bees.

Inside my hive of a house,
shuttered tight and saddened by loss,
I tear green leaves of pain and regret.
I ask: How can there be joy
when a child has died, yellow and waxy?

A part of me restlessly paces
the brown inter-locked tongue-and-groove floors,
shiny as spilled beeswax,
mirroring loss.
I notice my ashen, disinherited face,
the lack of sleep, the starved sadness.

In this world of white graves, there is borage—
little smears of soft blue-gray, tiny blue freckles.

In this dark house,
I am in diffused, light-blue light.

Outside, in the ashen air of the purple sunset
among webbed leaves transitioning
into red of nightmares,
there are bees
stirring in my heart.

I search into the distance
beyond the Depression-glass moon.

I am moaning for that one moment
when joy is brought back
from the brink of my breaking
into pieces tiny as blue-gray flowers.

How Love Works

How short we lay down time:
a summoning of daffodils
falling into disarray
as soon as they break open spring.

Yellow petals brown, droop, let go:
a fever breaking pitch. They break
hearts—fugues to loss.

I don't want to miss their impatience,
their days humming, light bending
through them, often repeating
until it doesn't: a transient passage.

It rained the whole time they opened,
speeding the process
and descent, witnessing
what never lasts.

Time never slows. Words and gestures
no one says. Daffodils come and go
and return, dependably, repeating
like a scratched, skipping record.
Time yellows the edges.

The daffodils keep trying to say something,
but words catch and fade into light,
a heart loosening its petals: let go,
let go.

III. Silence

"The quieter you become the more you are able to hear."
Rumi

In the Beginning

A flush of morning begins,
partial songs of awakenings.

I go out before the sun,
before the morning glories peek open
in moving shadows.

This is not the first time.
I hope it is not the last.

I am waiting for the moment
when the world slips away from now
into the unknown.

The air is weeping silently.

Whatever is held back
releases into absolute forgiveness.

Morning is rising and being pruned.
Sparks of light release.
Birds are relieved and begin to sing.

My life is being drawn
and written,
the ink hardly dry, and already
it seems almost over
on the way to starting all over again tomorrow,
hundreds of times,
always indecisive,
always uncertain,
corrected,
and revised.

The morning glories open.
Newborn birds wait to be fed.

The Spirit Moving the Silence

Listening inside that movement
to hear what is not spoken
but felt,

nothing seems to be there.

No one is there to whisper the words,
although they reside as memory
of water and birth,
a song that never ends.

We are distracted when we hear it.
Suddenly a dim room has light.

Do you hear
a sound less than ice forming
or a butterfly opening its wings?

What do you hear?

I see your head turning toward the words,
going quiet,
trying to focus on the source
and what it is saying.

I hear that voice, too.
It is urging *listen,*

listen.

When I Am with You

When I'm with you,
a body of stars starts to assemble,

light removes sharp edges
off shadows,

all love burrows deep.

When I'm with you,
I can lean off a bridge rail
in full moonlight.
Water shuffles underneath,
its unexpected reflection of love.

A breeze lifts leaves to see what is hidden.

Every delicate
loving touch
finds us deliberately.

Love spills out its song.

As wonderful as this all is,
love is pushed deeper inside
to make room for more love.

It is incredible to realize this is true.

We cannot speak about this without stammering,
without being truly amazed.

The Calling

The forest is summoning with absolute urgency,
inviting us into the thickest part
of the black-olive dark
tinged with a poignant green
intense with chlorophyll:

the Presence is waiting.

We can enter;
it is just a matter of longing
to be where we are meant to be.

We will be welcomed
for exactly who we are,
and we will belong.

This is never what we expect will happen,
but it does.
We are intended to fit in
even though we are unique.

The urging calls us.

When we respond,
stepping into that other world,
we will finally arrive
the way we were made to be.

Sitting Still to Hear the Quiet

If you listen, you can hear it—
a blackberry changing from flower
to berry in the slowness.

You can hear the leaves make oxygen
like filling a low tire
or a pinfeather breaking loose.

The stillness has different shades of quiet,
some potency, and then
words disappear.

You have to lower the heart
like temperature, like a stone
in molasses, filling the emptiness.

Arbor Day

All those yesterdays
just glare
silence afterward.

Hourly ocean waves ravish sand.

The world back then
seemed so impossibly immense,
chanting,
Come
rescue me.

One page from many mysteries—

a small offering was needed.

The world can feel
as overwhelming as a voice
never answering.

Holiness and the spiritual awakens
one greenness
in the purest hour,
a promise for a better day.

Love rivers
moving silence,
glitters of light
gurgling with excitement—

I understand this now.

Light emerges—
a heron
startling the water,

heart bolting
with flickering

stars weaving stories.

The Day Is Speechlessly Broken

The language of silence
slips secrets into the brink
of other places.

My deaf father scuffling
on a deer trail, winding
through white pine
into the shockingly
beautiful birds,
manifesting in trees
their music's long flight
he will never hear.

I sign *songbirds,*

signed *this*
is music.

Amazing Grace

My Amish grandmother never liked singing,
believing the devil encouraged the angels to sing
to test God's immense silence.

I caught her singing low
                        and slow,
        achingly broken sounds:
Amazing Grace   how sweet
        the sound   that saved
                a wretch
                                        like me
        lip-trembling   a hurricane
                humbled-to-death
                        by awesome-light
in the bluest sky with white-daisy-sun.

When the hidden voice
        from inside the silence spoke,
        she bent,
sang overflowing   sang
as if her life depended upon it,
as if everyone needed grace,
        and she had to relent
to God's infinite love,
        to this intense moment of surrender
        to love.

She noticed I had caught her singing,
        and she gave me a fierce look—
        let's-keep-this-to-ourselves.

I nodded   went back to my chores
humming   *Morning has broken*
        like the first morning   *Blackbird*
        has spoken

This One Blush of a Moment

We are crunching dry pine needles
in the contour of the land,
wind glittering with light rain,
tinking among the Douglas firs.

We stumble on an uneven path.

A banner of black-capped chickadees
chase from maple branch to branch
like there is no tomorrow.

Often, there is no certainty
there will be tomorrow.

Right now,
it is just this very good morning,
surging wind ushering in fall.

This one blushed moment
is all that we need.

Everything Is *Undoing*

Season's die-off begins its *not-knowing*.
Everywhere surrenders
to an illness—no one recovers.

Crickets ebb, throbbing heartbeat songs
about the heartlessness of these changes.

The ash laments,
its leaves tearing up.

The garden is bruised,
all its energy waning.

Gratitude of light declines.

I assure you this is all a lie,
but a neighbor has first-stage melanoma.
Another has early onset
like geese vacating the area.

No denial is allowed.
Our stories will ebb and flow
while a star goes dormant
in the margins of error.

A blighted tree is marked for removal.

Everywhere is changing.
It's frightening, watching it happen.

I cannot tell you this is acceptable
or that we should adapt
or follow the geese
to where the sky opens up
into forever.

A Mockingbird's Song

I keep trying to translate its message,
but someone keeps erasing
the scribbled clouds.

A rudimentary drizzle
in half-returning light
buckles against the hills.

The lacquered sky
pings water drops
down leafy stairs.

All during this,
love keeps approaching
as someone we've never met—

the one person missing in our life,
the one mystery
leaving us ecstatic.

The world is immutable—
the one sleep we wake from
in the peach-pink light of daybreak.

Centering

Whenever I feel I do not belong,
I listen to trees and rocks and small animals,
to their secretive,
meditative ways,
until I ripple,
enlarging and withdrawing,
hedging toward revelation.

Whenever I've been hauling
at invisible, unfortunate anchor,
I wait
until birds have eased into their songs.
Before morning opens its eyes,
breath expels from the earth,
and the hidden is seen.

There are still place like this,
places enriched by a spirit that renews.

People have run away from those places.

When I enter the sacred hush,
as soft as milkweed seed,
melancholy shakes out of me.
Stardust settles.

Light #2

The trace of light upon one branch
is never perfect,
but it is always unique,
moment to moment,
yearning to be seen,
to fulfill and be fulfilled.

Near Dawn

A thin wall of sound,
sudden intake, breathes
across the uneven forest.

You slept through this.

Far out on a stream,
there is yearning
for the wide unexplored
whorls of sunlight,

more stillness,
more gasp,
more we do not know.

We keep tugging at the ends of the unknown.

New Year's Day

At twenty degrees below,
air crunches
a weathered house's slats.
More snow is predicted.

I am out here in the edge of daylight to count birds
for the National Audubon Society
where, if you see one bird,
you estimate many more are hidden.

This is as inexact as counting stars.
There is no color,
no ambient light—
even the snow is dark.

A smattering of unreal red cardinals
in a snow-filled field
seems out of place
yet belonging.

An Unappeasable Need

After false starts of spring,
snow melts briefly
into brown patches.

Birds convene
in the return of light
on first piece of green.

Ravenous blue-black skies
open raven wings,
raining streaks of daylight,
entangled in branches
with tiny buds waiting
to burst into leaf-songs.

A swarm of blackbirds
are a week away from glances
of spring.

The Presence

I followed the path where light led me
to solitude,
opening a door of grief.

Birdsong hung in the air like leaves
I could pluck down.

Light leaves no footsteps,
but it enters me as a breathless whisper.

The empty shell of me fills,
light after light after light,
until I think I will shatter.

Paper Wasp

The skin of a paper wasp nest rips
like a map folded too many times.

A wasp shakes out in moonlight,
darkening,
the last moments
of a burned-out lightbulb
into a surer world.

Its wings curl open,
straighten
like wing-nuts,
rub simultaneously
before lifting toward
dawn just breaking.

It is indifferent
to what it brings,
and if I never move,
it will leave me alone.

I will not disturb this world.
It is too much like tissue,

easily broken.

Separation and Pulling Together and Separating

The body remembers what the mind forgets,
withdrawals from the world by inches,
escalating exponentially.

Wingspans of rainfall—
the body recalls, weeping,
the urgent calls for *more:*

blackouts more violet,
body, momentary vanishing,
someone inside.

A mouth is dangerous,
hands more so,
as they fling abandonment.

The mind subtracts stones,
water,
isolation.

Mind and body pass through elements,
separate,
still attached,

uncoupling,
coupling,
indecisive which is best.

Presence, 2

A sparrow landed on a branch,
barely moving the limb
with its heartfelt song.

We are never completely alone in this world.
There are reminders everywhere.

This can be a quiet world
even when there is a song
moving in a tall tree,

even if the melody hooks into my heart.
This can be a quiet place.

The bird solemnly sings,
stirring from branch
to sky to fence.

The pitch rises and falls,
tangles in vines,
becomes the black half-notes,
looking like pokeweed.

This is such a quiet,
quiet
world we live in.

When the sparrow goes away,
it takes its song with it.

This world can be a silent place.

Emptying

There is a certain amount of emptying
to getting anywhere.

In a way,
although these poems
came out of me,
spontaneously, as rain,
none of these poems
belongs to me
any more than rain
belongs to the clouds.

Final Leaf

In certain slowness,
the last leaf takes its final breath.

We do not recognize its fragility
is too much like our own.

We could lay our hands on that leaf,
just to feel it jolt out of its silent waiting,

this nearness of death,
this separation,

this world between living and dying,
the crossing-over and surrender.

We resist the temptation
to let go.

A Drop of Water

There is a drop of water among many
in the small bucket lifted out of a deep well.

The water experiences the wooden bucket,
the lifting into light of metal ladle and the quiet

silence and the experiences within silence
and the ones outside the silence, which are different.

A Single Water Drop

See the dew-burn-off,

the slowness of grass
as it stands, shaking
that weight,
shaggy droplets flinging
in slow motion.

It is then and only then
I know the world is alive.

I can see the drop
on a bulb move snail-like,
tentative,
like it might break,
and it wants to live
as long as it can.

We all want to hold together,
but every day, skin cells die
and flake off,
parachuting down,
and we have no choice.

The surface tension of a drop
can hold for long periods of time,
relatively speaking.

If careful,
I can stack one drop on top of another
before the entire structure collapses.

Inside that watery world,
smaller cells swim
secure in the knowledge
that their world is held together.

Some moments will fall apart
like that belief
that our small world
will not change.

Visualization

Walk under a waterfall
until enclosed by a curtain of water,

until water slows,
droplets like a strand of pearls.

The breaths between the drops
are faraway meadowlark songs.

Feel a drop
go through the molecules in your hand.

Silent Intent

Sometimes
an astonishment
bring us to our knees.

Some small detail can change
the way appearances
are translated into
surprising results
and silent purpose.

Alpine strawberries
work their silence
on a stump,
decomposing it
back into the music
of the earth.

This is what surrender looks like—

the release
and separation
into the unknown.

Music

Leaves fall out in silence
to the unknown,
depending on essentials
of sound,
touch,
sight.

Discover them
crinkling underfoot.

They were once firmly attached,
then let go
as light as an eyelash
heading into the understood
end of life,
fearless,
unburdened.

In death,
we all make our own music.

Acknowledgments

I would like to thank the following magazines in which a number of these poems have appeared:

Big City Lit: "Belonging"

Bitterzoit: "Nature"

Black Poppy Review: "Counting the Days," "Light," "Visualization," "When I Am with You"

Blue Heron Review: "Sitting Still to Hear the Quiet"

Border Crossing: "This Is Why I Plant Perennials"

Broadkill River Review: "Daffodils in Light"

Cloudburst (anthology): "New Year's Day"

Comstock Review: "The Distant Calling"

Flutter: "This Is How Light Works Where It Is Darkest"

Gyroscope Review: "On This Summer Day," "Within Reach of Purpose"

Houseboat (featured poet): "April 1," "Burning," "Crossing Over," "Emptying," "Healing in the Field," "Making"

Kentucky Review: "Final Leaf," "A Drop of Water"

Night Garden Journal: "Paper Wasp"

Nine Mile Magazine: "Borage," "Silent Intent," "Where Are the
Stars Tonight?"

Peacock Journal: "Dipping My Hand into a Cold Lake"

Pirenes Fountain: "Leaving Nothing Behind"

Poppy Road Review: "Field Study," "This One Blush Moment"

Red Wolf Press: "Music"

Seven Circles Press: "Light #2"

Soul-Lit: "A Mockingbird's Song"

Verse-Virtual: "New Dawn," "Revelation"

Your Impossible Voice: "Molecules," "Separating and Pulling
Together and Separating"

"The Calling," "In the Beginning" appeared in the mini-
chapbook, *In the Beginning* (Origami Poetry Project, 2020)

"A Single Water Drop" was selected as *Commended* in the
Cinnamon Press, International Single Poem Contest
(Cinnamon Press, 2015)

"Reflected Shade and Hint of Light" appeared in the anthology,
Mint Sauce & Other Stories & Poems (Cinnamon Press, 2008)

"The Sky Is Wide and Needs Filling" appeared in *Vanished into
the Impossible* (Origami Poetry Project. 2017)

About the Poet

Martin Willitts Jr is a retired librarian living in Syracuse, New York. He was nominated for sixteen Pushcart and thirteen Best of the Net awards. Winner of the 2012 *Big River Poetry Review's* William K. Hathaway Award; 2013 Bill Holm Witness Poetry Contest; 2013 "Trees" Poetry Contest; 2014 Broadsided Award; 2014 Dylan Thomas International Poetry Contest; Rattle Ekphrastic Challenge, June 2015, Editor's Choice; Rattle Ekphrastic Challenge, Artist's Choice, November 2016; Stephen A. DiBiase Poetry Prize, 2018; Editor's Choice, Rattle Ekphrastic Challenge, December, 2020. He won a Central New York Individual Artist Award and provided "Poetry on the Bus," which had forty-eight poems in local buses including twenty bilingual poems from seven different languages.

His twenty-four chapbooks include *Falling In and Out of Love* (Pudding House Publications, 2005), *Lowering Nets of Light* (Pudding House Publications, 2007), *The Garden of French Horns* (Pudding House Publications, 2008), *Baskets of Tomorrow* (Flutter Press, 2009), *The Girl Who Sang Forth Horses* (Pudding House Publications, 2010), *Van Gogh's Sunflowers for Cezanne* (Finishing

Line Press, 2010), *Why Women Are a Ribbon Around A Bomb* (Last Automat, 2011), *Protest, Petition, Write, Speak: Matilda Joslyn Gage Poems* (Matilda Joslyn Gage Foundation, 2011), *Secrets No One Wants to Talk About* (Dos Madres Press, 2011), *How to Find Peace* (Kattywompus Press, 2012), *Playing the Pauses in the Absence Of Stars* (Main Street Rag, 2012), *No Special Favors* (Green Fuse Press, 2012), *The Constellations of Memory and Forgiveness* (Seven Circles Press, web book, 2014), *A Is for Aorta* (A Kind of a Hurricane Press, e-book, 2014), *Pablo Neruda's Garden* (Finishing Line Press, 2014), National Chapbook Contest winning *William Blake, Not Blessed Angel But Restless Man* (Red Ochre Press, 2014), *Swimming in the Ladle of Stars* (Kattywompus Press, 2014), *City Of Tents* (Crisis Chronicles Press, 2014), *The Way Things Used to Be* (Writing Knights Press, 2014), *Late All Night Sessions with Charlie "the Bird" Parker and the Members of Birdland, in Take-Three* (A Kind of a Hurricane Press, 2015), *The Burnt-Over District* (e-book, Icarus Books, 2015), and *Martin Willitts Jr Greatest Hits* (Kattywompus Press, 2016), Turtle Island Editor's Choice Award for his chapbook, *The Wire Fence Holding Back the World* (Flowstone Press, 2016), *Nasturtiums in Snow Understand Green Is Coming* (Foothills Press, 2018), *You Enter, and It All Falls Apart* (Flutter Press, 2019).

His twenty-two full-length books include *The Secret Language of the Universe* (March Street Press, 2006); *The Hummingbird* (March Street Press, 2009); *The Heart Knows, Simply, What It Needs: Poems based on Emily Dickinson, her life and poetry* (Aldrich Press, 2012); *Art Is an Impression of What an Artist Sees* (Edgar and Lenore Publishing House, 2013); National Ecological Award winner for *Searching for What You Cannot See* (Hiraeth Press, 2013); *Before Anything, There Was Mystery* (Flutter Press, 2014); *Irises, the Lightning Conductor for Van Gogh's Illness* (Aldrich Press, 2014); *God Is Not Amused with What You Are Doing in Her Name* (Aldrich Press, 2015); *How to Be Silent* (FutureCycle Press, 2016); *Dylan Thomas and the Writer's Shed* (FutureCycle Press, 2017); *Three Ages of Women* (Deerbrook Editions, 2017); *The Uncertain Lover* (Dos Madres Press, 2018); *News from the Slow Country* (Aldrich Press, 2019); *Home Coming Celebration* (FutureCycle Press, 2019), 2019 Blue Light Award winner *The Temporary World*; *Unexpected* (Duck Lake Books, 2020); *Unfolding of Love* (Wipf and Stock Publishers, 2020), *Harvest Time* (Deerbrook Press, 2021), and *Meditations on Thomas Cole's Paintings* (Aldrich Press, 2021).

He is an editor for *Comstock Review*.

About the Artist

Minerva Miller is an artist and poet who resides in upstate New York. Their artwork and poetry have been on exhibit at the Everson Museum of Art, the NYS Fair, and the Rochester Contemporary Art Center. Minerva works in a variety of mediums, including ceramics, pastels, inks, charcoals, pencils, paints, and collage. Minerva enjoys being a part of the art community and volunteers at the Corning Museum of Glass and the Everson Museum of Art.

Title Index

V

W

First Line Index

www.ingramcontent.com/pod-product-compliance
Lightning Source LLC
Chambersburg PA
CBHW010729270326
41930CB00018B/3418